LADDER
TO THE
LIGHT

BETH
WOOD

MEZCALITA
PRESS

MEZCALITA PRESS, LLC
Norman, Oklahoma

Library of Congress Control Number: 2017918188

Cover Design: Jen Blair

MEZCALITA PRESS, LLC
Norman, Oklahoma

LADDER TO THE LIGHT

BETH WOOD

TABLE OF CONTENTS

HOME NOW. NOW HOME.

ACKNOWLEDGEMENTS

One night in Tsunami Books in Eugene, OR, I found a loose piece of paper tucked away on a shelf in the poetry section. It was the poem "Fear" by Lisa Rosen. Until that moment I had no idea that my fear was a tool and that I could use it as such. Thank you to Lisa Rosen and to the person who placed it there. Poets like Stephen Dunn, Jane Hirshfield, William Stafford, Mary Oliver, Brian Doyle have been whispering in my ear all along. For every whispered word, I am grateful. For every life raft, sliver of hope, cleansing tear. I have never needed it so much.

Deep thanks to Nathan Brown, Ashley Stanberry Brown, Mezcalita Press, and Jen Rickard Blair for bringing this book to life. Deepest thanks to you for reading.

On the days when the rest
have failed you,
let this much be yours—
flies, dust, an unnameable odor,
the two waiting baskets:
one for the lemons and passion,
the other for all you have lost.

~ *Jane Hirshfield, "Mule Heart"*

Truth is right where you are.

~ *Ruthie Foster, "Truth"*

LADDER
TO THE
LIGHT

PULLING
ON A PLOW

It Would Have Been Nice to Know

It's never about
the thing you think
it's about—

it's never money
(such a cheap
scapegoat)

or time or
sleep or sex. It's
about can you

be you, can I
be me once this
intoxication has

worn off entirely
and we are left
to scrub toilets,

arrange schedules,
pay bills. It's never
about that first

time you danced
in the kitchen,
lighter than air,

high on the feeling
of skin on skin, mouth
on mouth, heart

up against heart, that
feeling that somehow found
you in this shimmering

desert of doubt, you
believed it descended
upon you like a

windfall, a gift, the
publisher's clearinghouse
sweepstakes at your door,

when in fact that feeling
is your birthright. It
is already there in

every cell waiting, it
was always yours for
the taking, now take it.

THE THING YOU KNEW

On the second to last night sleeping
on your office air-bed
there blooms some sense of relief—

a hint that you may soon
have the ground beneath you again,
or at least something to resist

the weight of you. Everything
unraveling in cruel slow-mo:
time, what you thought this was,

busy-body grief. You fight the urge
in a relatively rare calm moment
to just ask point-blank, *Did you*

ever love me? knowing full well
the answer would be, *Of course*
I did, which, of course, means

the other thing—
the thing you knew
and wanted not to be true

(you did not want to know
but your body knew)—

the thing you knew but kept close
until the knowing broke you,
and then it set you free.

FORWARD MOTION

The poets are at it again.
Scattering their careful
whispers so that I will
stumble upon them at the
exact pinpoint moment
of need, crushing desire,
ache of new loneliness
pressed up against the old.
Oh Stephen Dunn, Oh Lisa
Rosen, what angels have
you become to speak
to me like this? What
blind magic? The knowing
hands you speak of—
that raft, tenderness,
deep cry like a prayer.
I am left with no choice
but to believe—to sigh
in wonder. What choice but
to write on these scattered
pages stained by coffee and
dust, to rise from another
sleepless night, gather my
awestruck heart into something
a builder could use, and dare
to never look back.

Green Dress

It's not wrong to want a green dress
for my birthday, I think, the deep

primal wailing of my shame
rising up like tendrils.

I could answer it with spring—a
sway in the hips, a nod yes. I could

answer it with silence, and yet here
is the celebration at hand, here

are the phone calls, cheerful songs.
I overheard the neighbor say it's

time to deadhead the roses. All I
could think of was the spinning

hippies and their abandon-
dance, pale spent petals littering

the ground all around me. All
I can do now is cry tears that

may never stop. Hold this ashen
moment like a seed. Let it go.

LESS HEAVY THINGS

If there comes a time
when my heartbrokenness is
westing, my grief receding,
and the lifecolor returns to my face,

remind me how I came to be here
unmasked, how I learned somehow
to endure each awful moment
one by one by one,

like climbing an impossible peak—
oxygen rare, human touch even more
rare still, the ground littered with detritus
from parties before, wounded seekers,

betrayed but climbing nonetheless, an
army of draught horses heads down,
pulling on a plow. Remind me there are
less heavy things. Bring me a feather

and let the wind, that divine jester,
blow it right out of my outstretched hand,
your eyes watching in wonder, no
words except yes and there you are.

GIRL IN SLOW MOTION

She never could settle in
for the motion of the world,
her knowing unfolding slowly
over time
like a seed sprouting up
or a mountain moving,

the entire scope of everyone
she knew, had
ever known,
flying past at the speed
of the day
her thoughts still hiding
in the dirt
waiting.

It's not too late, they say,
but their folded eyebrows
say something different.

They don't know
what she has squandered
wasted, grieved,

or maybe they do.

Maybe they've done
the same thing
at normal speed.

Maybe that makes it

easier to bear, to
sleep, to hide,

everyone
always running past.

She's only trying to
read their lips, decipher
in slow motion
what they are saying.

SALTED WORDS FROM THE FLOOR, TUESDAY

In the looming shadows of the deficit of language, let's revel for just a moment in the irony of talking about it. Every now and then when the clouds part, bursting pure radiance and bullseye precision of the perfect word, a sigh of relief, my tired heart swelling like it did before, back when I knew my name. On this particular Tuesday, I struggle to find the language to describe pain. The sports medicine doctor, too uncomfortably handsome for the size of this tiny room, asks me if it still hurts. *Well yes and no, I say. Sometimes. And now more of an ache on the right cliff's edge of my heel, whereas before it was the middle, but usually only in the morning or late at night.* He gives me a puzzled look. "How about when you run on the treadmill?" he asks. *Well funny you should say that because my foot didn't hurt then but my right hip did, kind of sharp, like a stabbing from the inside out.* "Hmmm…" he hums, utterly nonplussed. If this is a test, I have failed. If I am an archer, I have wasted all of my arrows. Self-mockery is my only option now. And furthermore, how to describe the other pain, the one of being alive? It hits me like a flying rock out of nowhere, walking by a photo I have passed by a thousand times, that cold day at the coast, suddenly my eyes stinging until I have no choice but to lie on the floor and leak salty water into my hair, this ground, breathe in deep all the way to my pitiful feet, remember your voice, wipe the water away, and then rise.

A HUMMING, SUNRISE

Ah, the thing that stays.
Then the impermanence,
that incessant turning,
the weaver at her wheel.
Sheep in the field asleep
standing up, dirty boots
piled into a corner. The
cold forgotten tea, quiet
whisper good morning,
that holy-shit sunrise with
her entrance forgivably late.
Frost on the ground, knife
chill in the air, birds huddled
on a wire, cat frozen like a
plaster-cast of feral hunger.
Blank page of day waiting
in silence, blank canvas of
night rolling up, sleep now
a forgotten memory, longing
like some humming held out
he feels in his chest all day,
all those telephone wires.
Mercy at the back door
knocking, no one home.

FORMING QUESTIONS

Do not let my absence
speak for me, let it be my
mouth, though as you know
it has been busy thirsting,
drinking, covering and un-
covering you. It would be
a mistake to claim anything.
There's no one here to claim.
And yet to dissolve into thin
air seems foolish. The way it
is foolish not to name every-
little-thing we see, that old
earthy, human enterprise. Do
not fear: I remember every-
thing, even the nameless,
and I see you from my open
window. You think I don't
know, but I always knew
root and vine, our bodies
forming questions, then
a minus sign.

MINUET IN G

1.

Well-meaning people DO mean well, I tell myself
over and over again, until this internal dialogue
becomes some kind of pitiful mantra. Truth is that
grieving mothers and widowers probably use it too
to talk themselves off that ledge of despair, the one
where no one in the world could possibly under-
stand what it feels like. And then I randomly strike
up a conversation with an acquaintance where I
actually tell the truth, and she bears her truth in
turn for me right then and there, therefore proving
I am in fact not alone, and I struggle to find the
words to thank her enough for what she has just
done. She shrugs it off and says you will do this for
someone someday, and that tiny seed plants itself
in the center of my chest, becoming the first living
thing to grow there in months.

2.

I often lie in bed in the dark wondering: what is a
reasonable hour for one to get out of bed and
make coffee? 5 am? Seems like anything before
that would be ridiculous, but then again think of all
the stuff one could get done before noon. It's hard
to go back to sleep with this giant wind turbine of
untethered logic turning in my beleaguered head.
Maybe I'll just get up and see what happens.

3.

In a completely transparent bid for attention and affection, I used to ask if he thought I was pretty. In frustration, he once told me he didn't believe in compliments, they were for weak people. Of course he didn't seem so averse to nice words before, as far as I can remember, but after so many years I guess all the words become some kind of blur, a swarm of bees that flies off in search of a better home. *Do you like my body?* I would ask in the dark and he said you just need to firm things up a little. Now that I am on my own the pounds seem to be melting off. For the first time in my life when I look in the mirror, I like what I see. Not one single ounce of shame where I was once covered in it. I never imagined this could happen and I have no idea what to do with this middle-aged windfall.

4.

Often around four in the afternoon I think to myself, *ok this will be the night that I don't drink wine.*

5.

Dear Bing search engine: I hate you. I just want
Google but can't figure out how to make it my
home page. So now when I want to search, I have
to type google.com. This kind of thing haunts you
when you live alone. But then again I would rather
live with Bing than someone who tailgates slow
drivers and flashes high beams at them to get the
fuck over, they have no business driving in the left
lane, who the hell taught them to drive anyway.

6.

I look at the clock and it's 6:30, therefore
answering the question—is it in fact socially
acceptable to get up at 4 am for no reason? I
conclude yes of course it is, as long as you do
important things like search for the term "minuet"
on Wikipedia and type out your inner thoughts
and musings in a caffeine induced frenzy for two
and a half hours.

7.

A social dance of French origin for two people,
usually in ¾ time. Adapted from the French *menu*
meaning slender, small, referring to the very small
steps.

8.

I've told myself for years I am a horrible dancer,
but the truth is that I love the feeling of moving
freely in my body. After all I did take Modern
Dance in high school and was not completely
laughed off the dance floor. I can still see our
instructor—a former ballerina in her seventies—
Lord knows how she wound up there, tight sleek
bun on her head, matte red lipstick every day, nude
tights, black leotard and pale pink skirts flowing
as she twirled and sashayed elegantly across the
floor. A wonder of grace and poise, a swan to our
flock of teenaged geese. I even got an A in that
class. I wonder what other stories I have been
telling myself on autopilot, a robot programmed
by her own erroneous thoughts. I may
have just found the override button.

9.

My best friend gives my number to Friendly Single
Dad in her son's class. She has become my social
coach as I cannot for the life of me figure out how
to talk to cute strangers. Dating sites are off limits
until I complete my women's self-defense class at
the community center. I meet FSD for a beer and
it's fun. He smiles a lot and actually listens to my
words, a revelation. Oddly enough his battle scars
are attractive. It's a new way of seeing things.

10.

The formality of classical music is the reason why I quit anyway. Still there is something strangely appealing about the order of it all. I sometimes dream of playing Bach's Minuet in G and wake up to the melody playing in my head, my fingers twitching in time. All those piano lessons. All those years. Embedded in my cells, my very DNA by now. A solidly engrained truth that the way to get better at something is to start slow, repeat often, and give over your focus until it becomes as natural as breathing. Small, slender steps. I realize that without even knowing it, I'm learning. I am taking them one by one.

Two Lonely People at the Same Time

A coincidence or a gift
floating on same waters,
separate rafts. A smile
as invitation or as
comfort, the raised
eyebrow of a question
at hand, two people
lonely at the same time.

I will set this burden down
for a moment, show you
a scar or three, drink in the
music you make late at night
in your room when no one
else is listening (I'm thirsty
and I'm listening now).

I'll tell you one thing no one
else within reason knows
and it slows the speed
of lonely for a time.

Is there anything I can do? you
offer kindly and my mind
races. Envelop me in your
arms, I think, hoping my eyes
are not windows. Take me
to bed, turn me over in your
palm like a treasure you found
in the dunes by that salty sea,

mouth on mouth, whispering
your exigent desire in my ear,
devouring me a little so there is
less of me to bear, I think.

Meanwhile I say *thank you,*
how kind, and I smile, take
one more sip of warm beer,
rise to hug you goodnight, grab
my sweater and go home.

HOLY WATER

Just as the dam is breaking,
calling out that old lawless
current, you heave a care-
fully negotiated breath,

imagine a girl scribbling
away by dim lamplight, art-
filled journal on her lap, nodding
off when her eyes grow heavy,

a spider or a weaver
making something out of nothing,
something else out of
every little thing,

unaware of what she would
squander, bow to, her spine a
flagpole, no country,

tiny raft on a river,

all those words lined up like bullets
reaching for the gun.

KOAN FOR BRIAN DOYLE

When the poet you love gets a brain
tumor, doesn't it change everything?

The one who writes in impossibly
symmetrical, rambling paragraphs
like some off-the-cuff old hermit
monk tending a high mountain
garden but with words, less with
purpose than with gentle intent.

When it moves you, and you let
out a sudden burst of air with a
"ha" attached to it, like laughing
but not funny, more like baffled
recognition of something you
already know, what then?

You feel they are instructions,
a manual for the present
moment, not to preach but
to notice, a quiet prayer.

Then when his friends ask,
What can we do? and he says,
*Laugh and be tender, more tender
than ever before*, those words you
have been waiting your whole
thirsty life to hear, what then?
Why the riddle? I think you
already know.

SARALYN'S MELODY

The birds are singing like every
day, like every day, some foreign
language that seems so familiar.

For heavensakes why are we here?
What have we come for but
to sing, fly some, sing again?

What ancient patterns do we answer to
never knowing we are doing
the answering, what accidental geometry

in this world where your geometry teacher—
the one you loved—can fall down and die
one summer day in Tennessee, just like that,

the one who said you had bright promise
when all you felt like was a giant blob of fat cells
and her words were a life-line, an offering,

the kind of kindness that turns the world.
Like a song at the beginning of the day,
a melody I'll never let go of or forget.

FIREFLIES ACCORDING TO LOIE

She tells me the fireflies
will most definitely show up—
they're just sleeping. They
have to rest their lights
so they can come back on,
light our way,
remind us to dance.

There must be one for every
tear. Maybe they even
outnumber them,
like stars.

Wait 'til you're old,
I say.
You stop counting.

Already I want
to take it back.

To the Well-meaning People Who Sighed and Said Well at Least There Were No Children

When I read the poem about
the two-dog nap, something in my
insides came loose, a tender
grieving ripple.

The older one fully white-faced
now—quiet, sneaky, mouth quick
and sure like a catcher's mitt. The
missing front tooth, the occasional
faint limp on the back right side,
appetite like a garbage disposal.
Ten to twelve years was their guess
but he just keeps on going and
going so who knows anyhow.
The young one made of dynamite,
possessing only two speeds: full-on
hurricane or passed-out snoring,
sometimes spread-eagle on his back,
feet in the air, eighty-five pounds of
breathe-in-and-sigh. The same color
as my coffee when I get it just right.
Green, unsure, impulsive, sometimes
bully, sometimes baby, galloping
after any round object like a
thundering herd of wild horses.

How we poured our love into them,
how we snuggled on the floor,

bought special food, walked twice
a day, went to manners class, private
lessons, took spontaneous trips to
the coast so they could see the water,
the wild expanse, the gleaming forever
sand, the look on his face when he
drank a mouthful. That same look on
my face now. So salty this truth, the
reason I cannot look back. These once
my babies, now somebody else's dogs.

Hey, It's Me

I'm just calling to say that I've thought about
calling so many times it seems rather absurd.
Hard to make the finger press the button in the
end. I know things are crazy there, I hope you're
hanging in. Yes, you envy my solitude but there
are things much worthier of your longing, dear.
I waste hot water and am ashamed it is the only
thing I have found to wash away the salt, thaw
my bones. Yes, it is still icy out here. Yes, I leave
tomorrow. Yes, I may have been drinking, though
not enough to forget I had it all once and let it go.
No soft landings after that, I am afraid. Broke all
my bones. I am a wooden doll now, the one
whose joints buckle when you press on that base
underneath, then release it and she stands back up.
I'm still standing. Call when you get a minute to
breathe? I have so much to tell you. I never
really had it after all.

WINTER SNAPPING (ONE THING SOFT)

I wanted to melt into softness.
My limbs felt weak. I heard the
voice that says, *Do the hard
thing, it is right*, the voice
beyond my knowing.

Maybe softness is for others
who need it more, maybe softness
was the womb, not the world.
Maybe that's the bargain. Maybe
we each and every one bargain
for a moment of softness here
and there. But oh to have it for
a string of moments, that's the
thing. Such sweetness. We bear
the weight of grief that piles on
one more brick each year, some-
times two. At the least my muscles
have grown strong. Down under
the sinew and bone is the girl that
asks for one thing soft. A puppy or
a ball of cotton or a rabbit-fur coat.

Winter air snapping tree limbs
like they were nothing, snapping
to its icy cold marching orders.
There was that one time. Surely
it must be enough.

OF GRIEVING

Then again, what do I know?
Damp winter air rolling
in off this mountain, I am
swimming in my cave through
grief of a love stillborn, a love
lost. Crowding around my
heater. And then I get the news:
my friend's daughter has died
by her own hand, he found her.
Who am I to grieve?
No one.
I know nothing.
I am a servant now
to his sorrow.
I bow down.
The mountain sighs
a breath of fog
and stays the same
in spite of everything.

THAT OLD FAMILIAR

I have held grief,
that old familiar
ball of twine.

I have carried that
woven basket of hopes
falling through cracks
and crevices

(hope a vaporous thing—
natural
helium
rising up
making your voice sound funny

slipping away
stillborn
falling on your feet
gone limp, you fear
no thing can hold it
now, no thing
can catch it).

But at least you hold
in your palm a string
that could wrap around
the world.

LITTLE MONSTERS

I am tired of talking, I think
to myself, the borrowed book
on introverts singing low
on my morning kitchen table.
All the ways we think are
broken, shameful, wrong
because we chafe against the
bright whirling world, the
carnival of secrets we keep,
corners where we place things
for safekeeping. Little monsters
hide there—our fear of laying
down stories we have bought
into hook line and sinker, and
told. *But I paid for them,* I think,
which is no reason to keep a
thing no longer useful. If you
keep it you will pay in different
ways. Every impulse now is to
whisper, to hum under breath
so every cell in my chest reverb-
erates, to nod and be understood,
or not. *I am tired of talking,* I think,
so much I almost say it out loud.

ROADKILL BUTTERFLY

At first I thought it was
a brown paper sack flapping
and fluttering there on this
Texas fried-egg blacktop.

Moving ten steps closer I thought
maybe it was a bird—one wing
sticking pitifully up like a shy raised
hand from the back of a classroom.

Five more steps and my jaw dropped—
a nut-brown butterfly or moth bigger
than my outstretched hand, right between
yellow lines, bathed in hot mortal wind.

And I know it's just a small thing.
But goddamn the windshield, our re-
ligion of the unholy engine, mean black
pavement, the fool behind the wheel.

BIRD'S EYE VIEW

Words move at their own
speed. A child's mind is surely
a floating thing, a balloon sailing
over deep canyons taking aerial
shots. From above she squints:
is that a crack, a crevice between
what she has been told and what
actually happens? *Do as I say, child,*
and so on. One day the seams do
not match up. *Family is everything,*
says the church youth leader who
gets caught in a wild embrace with
someone-not-her-husband at the
youth retreat, the suddenly furrowed
and questioning brows of teens now
the jury they both must answer to.
Thou shalt not steal but the lady in
the dumpster with no shoes picks
at it like a vulture. *Your grandfather
loves you* and he also kicks the dog.
To hold all these things at once
becomes the cracked window and
the diesel smell. Yes, we breathe new
air but now here is our work: to oil
the engine of the stories we must
tell as if our lives depend on them.

QUIET RIDDLE, 4:30 A.M.

If it begins with the moon,
let's say casting a shadow onto
your bedroom floor, then you give
a nod in wonder for that ghostly
light—not enough to disturb, just
enough to provoke a feeling
of looking back,

so then you are turned in
that direction. You might sigh
remembering a shared laugh,
you might kick yourself for
something you didn't say,

you're always not saying things.

In fact you might just lie there
listening to the creaks and whispers
of an old house telling you tales.

You hear music just before you drift
off to sleep. That's how you know you
are sailing behind that dark curtain. It's
different every time—once a symphony
of syrupy violins, once a lonesome piano
untuned, a choir of trembling voices.

And the moon just trickling in. Hell,
maybe it didn't begin there, who can say.

Where does a giant circle begin except
at the exact point you choose to look up,
breath in, and sigh out *hmmmmm*

MANY WAYS

There are many ways to begin,
not just paper and pen—
sometimes screen and puffy chair,
soft blanket, warm coffee,
old mug.

Many ways to grieve, she says,
and you reach back to recall
the pulsing river of tears,
the salted undercurrent
of everything, even now,

even when joy takes you
over, when you laugh out
loud unbelieving, when
pelicans in flight form-
ation are just too magical
to be true, their low dance
of symmetry almost too much
to bear, this water, these

laughing children, sharp
crackling sun, all of it
on the head of a pin.
There are many
ways to begin.

NOW HOME.
HOME NOW.

A TENDER BREED

One time you closed your
eyes to dream, and suddenly
you could carry that dream
by your side like a shield, a
swift magical curtain of relief
blocking doubt's searing sun.
You had no imagination for
this—could it have come by
chance, not by conjuring?

If you are one to believe
in chance you might get
some sleep. And if you don't
then you are a tender breed,
as you've always known, as
have all those around you.

But one day you woke
up thirsty, put on the
kettle to boil, ground the
coffee, drank the poet's
words as a sacrament,
and decided you deserved
some tenderness in return.

Corpus Christi

Bone-white shell pressed up
against stone. Tide, that deep
raider of time and sand, you
wonder in the interim if you
should don a costume, a mask.
An unrelenting crow outside
your window negotiating with
the way things are. Unbelief
is a silk robe now, a flowing
sleeve, a loosened hem. Ev-
erything altogether unraveled
into what it sang into being
in the first place. Now home.
Home now. Brightness our
reward among the rippling
echoshocks of disappoint-
ment. Tastebuds burgeon-
ing into some thing whole,
some thing complete—not
just sugar now, bittersweet.

THANKSGIVING DAY PRAYER

For this day I bow down and give thanks.
For yesterday and each yesterday that came before.
For the blessings that are obvious and for
the good sense to recognize and celebrate them.
For the blessings that are downright ugly,
the lessons learned the hard way, well of
cleansing tears and grief, necessary counter-
weight to joy. For the blossoming of flavors on
my tongue and for the savoring. For these dear
humans who created me and raised me with intent,
and for their good health. For the love that is alive
in my heart, for the ability to give it away and
never empty it out, and for the grace to receive
it, too. For all who share my blood and for all who
are gone. For dear friends (chosen family) and our
priceless laughter, shared sorrow, bright joy. For
the hands that forged these utensils, the hands that
grew and prepared this food and for all the life-
force that has gone into this very meal. For the
knowledge that this moment is all we have. For
this breath and for the next I give thanks.
Cinnamon, salt, cranberry, thyme, this
is what gratitude tastes like.
Amen.

ONE MORE DAY

Oh this body, give
me one more day. Let
me caress a lover until
we tangle my hair in
jewelry, lie in tall grass
watching marshmallow
clouds go by, buy fresh
things from farmers,
transform them in my
kitchen, breathe crisp
winter air and gasp as it
burns these lungs. Watch
that damn cat watching
songbirds all day through
clear glass. Stay in other
houses when I cannot find
my own. Find joy and give
it away, stand in the middle
of the street kissing, bring
in the mail, lick the bowl,
walk on crimson leaves
while the trees in perfect
symmetry sigh. Bake the
bread, wear the dress, dig
up grandmother's recipe
and feed my friends, sing
because it feels good, sing
because I can, sing until I
remember, then dance, hug,

pray, bow down, know this
is enough, hold on to the
knowing, sing some more.

OLD HABITS DIE AND THE SKY
DOES NOT FALL IN

Goodgrief I can't believe
how "lucky" as they say,
although it's without a
doubt not luck at all.

Every cell lit up
and humming with
gratitude. After all
would you look at

this roof, these books
filled with pain-stakingly-
thought-out words, those
eggs in the kitchen,

each one perfectly im-
perfect, perfectly given,
sun peeking through sy-
rupy yolk of Oregon fog.

For godssake, look at
all this. Embarrassment
of riches, except I'm not
embarrassed anymore.

I could jump for joy, or
I could stand up now,
take my clothes off for
all to see, make this

body a prayer, the
prayer it has always
been underneath the
old habit of asking.

At the Corner of Soybeans and Corn,

it's not enough to say,
*Thank you Minnesota infinite
sky.* Rays like fingertips in
the dirt, monarch mileposts,

a crooked roadkill snake,
pelican and cormorant
circling, searching
for a place to land.

I must also say,
Thank you legs for
carrying me (feet
for being arrows),

for this feeling I could
go on forever—this
golden nowhere road.

I have seen your fields
in winter—cruel
sharp and desolate,

but this. This must be
the time of forgiveness

this must be the long view,

fertile ground for a seed to
push up, thrive, drink, sex,
blossom. Something

to hold on to.

RETIREMENT PLAN

To have next to nothing
is a relief at times,
laughable at others.

Things don't matter...
people do, my grandmother
would say, followed by
If I can't eat it drink it
or rub it on, I don't want it.

Amen! A hallelujah
chorus running three
generations back.

Even from a rusty
old chair on her dusty
tumbleweed frontporch
she knew if things do not
serve us we serve them.
It's tricky that way...

which is why I invest
only in books of
poetry now, not
the stock market,
not the future.

Only one of these is real.

I MET A MAN

who turned me over in his
palm like a coin, then placed
me right back in his pocket,
it was so very dark in there.

I've never been flat before,
but it was lovely for a time.
(I may have also been shiny,
but I have no way to tell.)

I landed tails up on the side-
walk outside the littlecafe he
always goes to before meetings,
he gets so hungry you know.

I want to shout *Wait!* as he
opens the lime green door with
a brass bell tied to it, but as you
also know I have no mouth.

A stranger might crouch down
and pick me up. His very pos-
ture confirming this: the natural
resonance of forgotten things.

Here comes the old woman with
a tea cup dog. I am back now to
all my dimensions. Funny how
he never thought to spend me.

LETTER TO MY FRIEND PETER MULVEY

Dear Peter,

Thought you should know that the combo of
listening to your album "Silver Ladder" at top
volume while driving through Wyoming with
the windows down in the summer is simply
exquisite. The wind in your hair, white lines
whipping in underneath you, sky coming at
you at 82 MPH, clouds making shadows and
antelope sometimes standing in them.

Track 6 is especially tender while the hawk
swoops down. And track 11, well that is a
flat-out trip. (Do you really have that dream?
I'm wondering what you eat late at night?
The woman is my favorite part, the sigh
in your voice.)

You stop for gas as there is so much nothing-
ness you fear running out, the blue heeler
puppy with a purple bandana in the parking
lot with his ears pinned back, frightened of
motorcycle sounds. The boy on a bike, his face
caked with dirt, riding in circles with a bag of
groceries hanging from the handle. Nothing
on earth more important than this. Not time,
not the beloved earring that fell off somewhere
between Sheridan and here, not the impending
sandwich, not the cold beer waiting at the end
of this long driving day. Everyone always asking,

how do you keep going? Aren't you exhausted?
When the truth is there are unseen things boiling
up in your heart as you realize, wide awake, you are
running toward something now, not away from it.

A Woman Will Stand and Sway,

a gentle rocking with no boat
and no water. Some ancient
lullaby threaded through the
metronome of hips. Pendulum
of flesh to quiet the cries of
babies never born, already
born, not born quite yet. Her
breast an offering even to
a lover to fill the mouth,
quench the thirst, pacify the
restless animal living in his
every cell. She will recognize
pain without words, wrap
herself around it, wrestle
it to the ground, tender
warrior. She needs no
bullets, knives, drones—
she absorbs them, unthreads
the needle of violence done in
the name of anyone, anything,
and sews instead a warming
quilt. She harvests the garden,
hears faraway music often and
without warning sees the child
in us each by each, humming
a quiet tune underneath her
breath for the broken ones.

Our Jewel in the Dark

I found a pebble shaped
like a heart lodged between
city sidewalk cracks, bent
down to pick it up and
heard you laughing, this
moment all of a sudden
revealing its ancient
alchemy.

Of course I saw it there

(darkness already descended).

Of course your boot heel
grazed that knobby tree
root bursting from mute gray
concrete, turned your ankle just
enough to tip your tipsy body
over into mine.

A shower of giggles, we hold
on, lean back, howl it to
the moon, silent witness to
our joy.

I bend back over
to catch your fall, catch
my breath,

and find it there.

THE ROAD

I don't mean to be cryptic
but words can have teeth,
sometimes glances too,

a quiet fire beneath the
surface you think you have
seen but there is more to tell,
more I am burning to tell you.

I can simmer under the radar
until you ask. The feeling
that you forgot something,
or what you think you saw
in your peripheral vision:

that's me waiting it out—
godknows I can be very still
when I need to, it's simply
a matter of blue on blue.

I don't mean to be cryptic
but there is a silk thread
from me to you. You never
noticed it was there before,

thin as a whisper, still
there, after, a ripe and
tangled relic in between.

I don't mean to be cryptic
but your skin is the road
I must travel on, walking
toward you now
and away from you
at the same time.

LOVER'S PRAYER

Ohlord please bring me a lover
who won't hold on too tight,

who will see my scars and not
recoil, who will trace them with
a single index finger and wonder
aloud how they got there,

who'd be satisfied with the silence
that follows, or the answer,

who will drink my sudden tears
grateful for the weather, the salt,
thirsty for clear water streaming
just underneath my skin.

Let him be patient, Ohlord, to
the infinite whims of my desire,

let him be hungry enough to
groan and make faces only
shared pleasure can conjure,

let him forget himself for those
otherworldly hours, let him set
down the weight, let me be
weightless in his good company,

let me take him flying above vast
cities, jagged shores, pillowy clouds

for just a tiny little while so he can
remember that rush of feeling on a
cold, rainy, cruel and crushing day,
take it with him tucked in his wallet

let it be useful to him, Ohlord, a
holy balm, even after I am gone.

My Valentine

My valentine is a bird
high in these old trees
singing for a reason I cannot know
so tiny I cannot find her.

My valentine is the rain
covering this city like a grandmother shawl
giving us time and occasion
to appreciate young sun.

My valentine is the quiet,
something earned, earthy and
sweet, now never to be
taken for granted.

My valentine is the pen,
the page, the guitar
in the corner, words my
paint colors for blank canvas.

My valentine is my eyes
bringing me beauty, dreaming it up
out of nothing, imagining the shape
of a tiny bird singing,

the reason for the singing
maybe I do know after all,
the living Yes is the reason,
the song my valentine.

Instructions on Winning

Once you mentioned how you love to walk
down a busy street side by side, her beauty
a thing not possessed by her, but instead pro-
jecting ahead of her like a soundwave, invisible
music she cannot hear. You were dancing to it.
Then you said you feel like you have won her.
She considers this and smiles.

She took your hand in hers by surprise to both
of you one spring afternoon, you held it like a
dove and released it just when it was time. You
walked to the wrong restaurant, laughed, drove
halfway across town to sip noodles in a park,
marveled at the old man and his frisbee dog,
laughed some more, showed her your old
neighborhood by happy accident.

You take her to a green hillside with a blanket
and wine, listen to her words, all of them, how
they spill out like magic scarves, then you listen
to the colors in between. You hold her gaze until
you cannot stand it one more minute, and then
you kiss her. You never stop kissing her. Throw
in a silly joke or three.

In case you have wondered, this is how you win
the girl. Let her gather herself. Forge a cup for
your longing and let it overspill from time to time.
Know when to be tender, exactly when not to be.
For goodness sakes hold her. Repeat until her
sorrow fades, a balloon carried away on the wind.

This is how you keep on winning the girl. You keep doing this and also do all that you know to be right, even and especially when it is most hard, even and especially when no one is watching.

This is how you win the music, the dance, the crowded street, the heart inside of the girl you keep on winning.

A Song for Ashley

My friend wrote a book called
My Salvaged Heart, and I am
filled with joy that he feels this

way (his was not an easy road).
Makes me think of a junkyard, a
certain svelte, determined some-

one picking through the rubbish,
finding worth and grace in that
tiny little rusted orb somebody

else threw away, paying cash to
that grumpy yard attendant, walk-
ing away with gold in her pocket,

smiling 'cause she got it for a song.

THOUGHTS ON A CARTOON GUITAR BOOKMARK

I wanted you to have this, said my seven-year-old niece as she handed me a bookmark with a multi-colored cartoon of a guitar on it. Not like the kind I play, mind you, but close enough. She used her allowance to buy it, her mother says just then, puffing out her bottom lip in the universal gesture of *isn't-that-so-sweet*, to which I instinctively do the same, multiple layers of cotton-candied delight washing over me. That she loves the bookstore so much as to lose herself in it. That she stood among the books and thought of me. That she valued that thought so as to want to mark it with something physical. That she parted with two of her dollars to give that thought to me. That she has done what a child will do so many times I have lost count. They dance up to you in a blue tutu, spilling over with giggles and curls, hand you something nonsensical, light you up, and then dance away. Never knowing you will save this shining moment, use it later in the dark. Meanwhile she's still dancing.

THE DRIPOLATOR, SUNDAY, 7:30 A.M.

A deep south coffee shop on Sunday
is a ghost town. So welcome to these
ears tired of all professing. Three salt
and pepper men sit in the corner whis-
pering words—I assume Bible study—
but further into my eavesdropping I
recognize they are sharing poetry. "I
wrote this last July, just before Mom
fell," I overhear. Grown men offering
up careful internal weavings right here
in public. I smile into my coffee cup.
I am convinced the world can go on.

Songwriters Workshop, Sunday Afternoon

We sit around in a circle, drink
coffee and talk about it,
do silly exercises, delight each
other with our creations.

We talk around it, we make
lists. We discuss form, melody,
the way the voice lifts in that one
spot, how the spine shivers.

I'll be honest: it does matter
what pen you use. If you're
even a pen person. Or maybe
you write on the iPad now—

that bright white screen forming
a dividing line between those who do,
who don't. We want to understand
it all yet we never do, yet we march

on. Every single one of us in awe
of the divine mystery. Every one of
us struggling to make the pen move
(or the cursor). Every one in love.

Mother's Crown (I Like Birds)

Where do you get your curls?
people always ask me and I point
to her, not knowing how to answer

factually, knowing I didn't
do much, actually I didn't do
anything at all. She is

mostly wavy now, silver
crown on her head, but she
passed them along like

a secret shared between us.
I used to despise them, iron
them, spray them down into

sticky submission, a fool's
endeavor, oh they never minded
me anyway. On my worst days

it's like a bird's nest is
parked on top of my head—
I don't mind really—

I like birds. On my best days
they do quietly what they
were meant to do all along.

I let the question hang
in the air. She looks my way.
I smile for both of us.

BIRDS OF THE NORTHWEST

My mother makes lists
of birds. Fifty-eight names,
each beside a number, tucked
inside a trusty field guide she
accidentally left on her last visit.
Titled "Oregon Bird List," it
begins: 1. Pied-billed Grebe
2. Double-crested Cormorant
3. Great Blue Heron and so on,
brought to a close by 58. Downy
Woodpecker. My father wrote
51 through 56. Then here is our
trip to the coast in 41 through
47: Brown Pelican, Pacific Loon,
Surf Scoter. Oh what rainy-day
joy to find such a thing. What
joy in keeping a list of beautiful
things we have tried to capture
with the tattered net of language,
often falling short. What joy her
cursive, the readiness of her delight.
A rush through these tired veins:
blooming curiosity, memory, rev-
erence for blind weaving. The next
time a Song Sparrow scratches and
chimps in the dirt mixed with leaves
outside my window, I'll reach
for pen and paper, and write.

COWBOY ELEGY

When the Zen cowboy
opened his mouth it was
like whiskey and honey,
deeply worn saddle on
a sure-footed chestnut
hoofing home from a
long driving month, only
three more miles to go.
Around the spitting fire
we bathed in it, the warmth
of his song. His right hand
keeping its ever-steady gait,
jaw and cheekbone rugged
steep canyons, whimsy some-
where in his eyes, his bald
crown lit up from the inside,
singing for his supper and
then some. *Great song, kid*,
he said, and he tipped his hat
in my direction, assuring me
at last that I belonged, a tiny
gift that lingers still like the
smell of wood smoke and
warm horses. I guess he heard
a dinner bell ring, we fell asleep,
and now he's gone on home.

Sympathy in Music

The color of shame must be red,
right? The sheer flush of it creeping
up your spine, setting your neck on
fire, mussing your hair. For wanting
what you want, you get voices, each
one from the outside not knowing a
single thing about you but shouting
all the same. For wanting what you
want, well you must be filthy. Crawl-
ing into a dark hole like an earthworm
seems like a decent solution, all things
told. For wanting what you want, his-
tory sings to you, a broken hymn or
a moan, every other soul who wanted
to crawl into a hole now a chorus res-
onating at the same frequency. In
music they call that sympathy and
it makes perfect sense. For wanting
what you want, you may face sharp
teeth of hateful words from strangers
who have forgotten that tender little
being that lives inside us all. Then again
you may find comfort in the hole you
have crawled into, decorating it with
string lights and paper flowers given
by children who still smile and run
toward you when you walk into a room.
For wanting what you want, you are
human and pulsing with life, and no
voice or hymn or hole can keep that

from you, no shame. After all you will
return to mother earth who will rise
to meet you in spite of what you want.
You will dissolve. Until then listen, keep
teeth at bay and keep on wanting. For
goodness sakes walk toward anything
that hears your song and says Yes.

THE WAY

Stark competing impulses clash all the time:
Oh lord, I want the sandwich, but I should
eat the lettuce, no dressing. You want the
quick zip home, but you should take the
winding forest path so your mind can do
its own unfolding of wings under water.

We want love to be the question and the
answer, but the truth is that it says come
closer get away from me, all at the same
time. If you turn around to glance over
your shoulder, well forget about it already.

It can't be the question or the answer, only
the way, and that shocks like hot coals until
you step back, take stock, look up at the stars,
admit you are lost, and damnit keep on going.

LLANO ESTACADO

Yes, I have a mule heart
a spider heart
a long-black-snake-in-the-henhouse heart
a cotton-lining-the-side-of-the-sun-scorched-
highway heart
and all that just before sunrise

I stand firm in gravity
watching her work
pulling eggs when no one is looking
a quiet memory of persistent vastness, the infinite
plains that shaped my seeing

I love what I love
wake up and start weaving
slither to another woodpile of words
give my song to this painterly sunset, lie down flat
in surrender, begin again.

AUTHOR BIO

Beth Wood is a poet and award-winning singer-songwriter who has toured the country playing music and delighting audiences for twenty years. She has released ten independent albums and one book of poetry, *Kazoo Symphonies* with Mezcalita Press. Joy is the currency that runs through Beth's work, through story and song, and her sensitive, intuitive nature allows her to address sorrow in a way that resonates and moves audiences and readers. Beth's work has expanded to include teaching and song coaching, as well as leading workshops at festivals, and songwriting retreats.

MEZCALITA
PRESS

An independent publishing company
dedicated to bringing the printed poetry,
fiction, and non-fiction of musicians who
want to add to the power and reach
of their important voices.

CPSIA information can be obtained
at www.ICGtesting.com
Printed in the USA
LVHW091956170419
614605LV00002B/188/P